G000060271

VASSILIOS SPATHOPOULOS

Scientific Secrets of Edinburgh and Glasgow

Places to explore, cafes to discover

Copyright © 2019 by Vassilios Spathopoulos

All rights reserved. No part of this publication may be reproduced, stored or transmitted in any form or by any means, electronic, mechanical, photocopying, recording, scanning, or otherwise without written permission from the publisher. It is illegal to copy this book, post it to a website, or distribute it by any other means without permission.

Vassilios Spathopoulos has no responsibility for the persistence or accuracy of URLs for external or third-party Internet Websites referred to in this publication and does not guarantee that any content on such Websites is, or will remain, accurate or appropriate.

First edition

This book was professionally typeset on Reedsy.
Find out more at reedsy.com

To those who travel to learn

Contents

Foreword

For additional information including a map presenting all the scientific sites and recommended cafes, please visit the companion website at: https://mysciencewalks.com. Also, as opening times and entrance fees can change, they are not included in the guide and should be obtained from the venue websites.

Preface

For a small nation, Scotland has provided an impressively large contribution to the development of science. In fact, a detailed presentation of its scientific achievements could not be performed within the limits of a short guide. This work has been written as a taster and it is hoped that it will provide you with the impetus to further research a fascinating subject. The author has lived in both Edinburgh and Glasgow for almost half his life and loves travelling and writing about science. While on trips he also enjoys seeking out hidden cafes that help him relax and digest his new discoveries. This compact scientific guide to Edinburgh and Glasgow combines all the above passions. It introduces you to lesser known aspects of the history of science, such as the Scottish astronomer who was the first to measure the distance to a star, and at the same time takes you to where famous scientists that shaped our modern understanding were born and flourished. It also recommends museums with scientific themes, planetariums and star observatories. For each site introduced, a nearby cafe is suggested as one of the author's favourites. A map is provided on the companion website (https://mysciencewalks.com) with the locations of all cafes and places of interest. If you are a keen traveller, with an interest in science and also enjoy a good cup of coffee, this guide is definitely for you.

James Clerk Maxwell's Birthplace

Background:

Edinburgh is the birthplace of one of the greatest scientists of all time and although many visitors will have heard of the likes of *Newton* and *Einstein*, few will be familiar with the name of **James Clerk Maxwell**. Most physicists, on the other hand, would rank Maxwell alongside the above mentioned giants of physics. In fact, there was no greater admirer of the man than Albert Einstein himself, who kept a portrait of the Scot in his office and who once remarked that: *"One scientific epoch ended and another began with James Clerk Maxwell"*.

Young Maxwell at Cambridge University

James Clerk Maxwell was born in Edinburgh's New Town, at 14 India Street, on the 13th of June 1831 and was brought up on the family estate at *Glenlair*, near Dumfries in southwest Scotland. His father had been born "John Clerk", adding the surname Maxwell to his own after he inherited a country estate from connections to the Maxwell family. The young James' quest for knowledge was evident from when he was a young boy. In a letter to her sister his mother Frances states that:

"He is a very happy man, and has improved much since the weather got moderate; he has great work with doors, locks, keys, etc., and "show me how it doos" is never out of his mouth. He also investigates the hidden course of streams and bell-wires, the way the water gets from the pond through the wall".

His mother was also his first teacher, but she unfortunately died when he was only 8 years old. His father subsequently hired a young tutor, but Maxwell quickly got bored with him, to the point of one day grabbing a tub and paddling to the middle of a duck pond in order to escape from his tutor's instructions. His rebellion paid off and when he was 10 years old was sent back to Edinburgh to attend school and live with his aunt.

When Maxwell appeared at the *Edinburgh Academy* (still functioning today) his country boy appearance was the subject of mockery from his new classmates and he soon acquired the nickname "Dafty". That changed when his academic capabilities started to show. Astonishingly, he wrote his first scientific paper when he was just 14. One of his father's friends, Professor *James Forbes* read the paper to the Royal Society of Edinburgh, as James was too young to present it himself.

In 1847 at the age of 16, he enrolled at Edinburgh university and when he was 18, he published another two papers which he was once again deemed too young to present at the Royal Society himself.

In 1850 he moved to Cambridge University where he distinguished himself as Second Wrangler and joint winner of the prestigious Smith's prize for his performance in mathematics. During his Cambridge years he was in frequent contact with many outstanding undergraduates who at times would visit his room seeking his mathematical advice. Maxwell had a good sense of humour which is illustrated by the following story. One evening friends were in his room and he started spinning one of his famous spinning tops. When his friends left, the top was still spinning. Early the next morning, Maxwell noticed one of the friends coming towards his room, so he set the top spinning again, and returned to bed, giving the impression it had spun all night. As a result of this prank his top became legendary.

In 1856, the year his father passed away, Maxwell became Professor of Physics at Marischal College, Aberdeen. Still only 25 years old, he was at least 15 years younger than most of his colleagues. Although busy with organising his teaching (which included weekly evening lectures to working men at the Aberdeen Mechanics' Institute), he carried on with his scientific work that included the publication of a breakthrough paper on the theory of gases. His research on the stability of Saturn's rings (a problem that had eluded scientists for 200 years), resulted in his being awarded the prestigious Adams prize, further enhancing his reputation. Aberdeen also brought him good fortune in his personal life as he got married to the daughter of the Principal, Katherine Mary Dewar, in 1858.

In 1860 he left his native Scotland once again, this time appointed to the Chair of Natural Philosophy and Astronomy at London's King's College, where he carried out some of his most important scientific works. He was awarded the Rumford medal for his research on colour vision and in 1861 produced the world's first ever colour photograph which he chose to be of a tartan ribbon, a tribute to his native country. He also continued to publish extensively on the behaviour of gases. It was, however, his work on electromagnetism that would eventually elevate him to the status of Einstein and Newton.

What Maxwell did, in simple words (building on the work undertaken by scientists such as *Michael Faraday*), was to suggested that light, electricity and magnetism could all be explained in a single electro-magnetic theory. His final paper on the subject, "*A Dynamical Theory of the Electromagnetic Field*", was written in 1864 and is considered one of the most important papers ever published in physics. Not only did it explain electromagnetism, but it also provided inspiration to 20th century scientists leading to the development of theories such as the theory of relativity and quantum theory.

In 1865 Maxwell resigned the chair at King's College and returned to Glenlair with his wife Katherine. He stayed there for 6 years producing research papers and books on topics such as heat theory and engineering. In 1871 he returned to Cambridge to become the first Cavendish Professor of Physics and was put in charge of the development of the *Cavendish Laboratory*, which eventually became one of the most important research hubs in the world.

James Clerk Maxwell died at the young age of 48, in 1879. His remains were brought back to Scotland and buried beside those of his parents in the ruins of the old Kirk, at the village of Parton (close to Glenlair).

The scientific debt owed to "Scotland's Einstein" is immense. In his short life he managed to publish five books and about 100 scientific papers covering an astounding number of topics. It is from his theory of electromagnetism, however, that most of modern technology stems. For this contribution to science the unit of magnetic flux, the *Maxwell*, has been named after him. Radio, television, mobile phones and many other inventions we now take for granted, all work on the same principle, the propagation of electromagnetic waves at the speed of light. It is why the famous 20th century physicist *Richard Feynman* said that:

"*From a long view of the history of mankind, seen from, say, ten thousand years from now, there can be little doubt that the most significant event of the 19th century will be judged as Maxwell's discovery of the laws of electrodynamics*".

The site:

Maxwell's birthplace is a terraced house built for his father in 1820. The *James Clerk Maxwell Foundation* founded in 1977, acquired it in 1993. The original character of the house has, to a large extent, been preserved. Minor alterations have been made primarily for converting the former dining room into a small museum. The museum displays memorabilia such as portraits, manuscripts and books associated with Maxwell, his family and his scientific contemporaries.

Maxwell's Birthplace

It is possible to visit the house (admission free) and one hour tours are conducted every Tuesday. For more information on the site and how to organise a visit, check out the website: http://www.clerkmaxwellfoundation.org.

A 15 minutes' walk from his birthplace, at the eastern entrance of George Street, there is a statue of Maxwell together with his beloved dog Toby, a fitting tribute to the greatest scientist ever born in Scotland. A Charitable Trust has also been established to conserve and preserve the family home of Maxwell at Glenlair (a 2.5 hr drive from Edinburgh). A visitor centre has been set up and visits can be arranged through the *Glenlair Trust* website: http://www.glenlair.org.uk.

Maxwell's Statue in Edinburgh

Where to find it:

James Maxwell's birthplace is located on 14 India Street, in Edinburgh's New Town.

Where to digest your knowledge:

Nestled conveniently between Maxwell's birthplace and Edinburgh Academy where he attended school, **Leo's Beanery** is a family run cafe serving excellent coffee and tasty, fresh food.
- **Address:** 23A Howe St, Edinburgh EH3 6TF
- **Website:** https://www.leosbeanery.co.uk

Did you know?

Maxwell also enjoyed writing poetry, much of it influenced by his scientific work, such as the following:

"O look! how queer! how thin and clear,
And thinner, clearer, sharper growing
The gliding fire! with central wire,
The fine degrees distinctly showing.
Swing, magnet, swing, advancing and receding,
Swing magnet! Answer dearest, What's your final reading?"

Calton Hill Observatory

Background:

The famous Scottish novelist, *Robert Louis Stevenson,* summed it up when he said that *"of all places for a view, this Calton Hill is perhaps the best"*. **Calton Hill**, has always been a magnet for visitors both for its breathtaking views of the city and for the impressive monuments that lie scattered on its summit. How many of these visitors are aware, however, that this site is in some way associated to a holy grail of astronomy? Or that one of its famous astronomers also inspired a cult believing in the mystical powers of Egyptian pyramids?

The story is one that begins many thousand miles from Edinburgh, at the Cape of Good Hope, South Africa. It is where the Scottish astronomer, *Thomas Henderson,* was appointed H.M. Royal Astronomer in the year 1831. Born in Dundee in 1798, he began his career as a lawyer's clerk, before his passion for astronomy eventually led to his appointment. Although complaining of the difficult working conditions (from defect telescopes, to having to check for snakes under his bed), he made a substantial number of astronomical observations during his time at the Cape. After just over a year, however, he decided he had endured enough of the "dismal swamp" as he called it, his frail health being affected by the local climate. His predecessor had died from scarlet fever and was actually buried in the observatory grounds, so Henderson returned to Scotland probably trying to avoid a similar fate.

During his last month in South Africa, intrigued by the observation made by another astronomer, *Manuel Johnson* based on the south Atlantic island of St Helena, that the star *alpha Centauri* (technically a star system) which is the closest to our solar system, exhibited a substantial change in its position relative to other stars, he focused his work on this discovery. What he was primarily interested in was the detection of a *parallax* for alpha Centauri, the apparent change in position of an object when viewed from different vantage points. As our planet moves around the sun, the view we get of a star changes ever so slightly during the year as it appears to move relative to its background. The fact that alpha Centauri seemed to exhibit a measurable movement, suggested that a parallax effect might be at play.

Importantly, by obtaining the parallax of an object, it is possible to estimate its distance (the closer the object is to the observer, the greater the parallax). As stars are at an immense distance from us, their parallax is extremely small and is not detectable to the naked eye. Ever since antiquity, astronomers had been trying, without success, to detect this subtle effect. Nineteenth century telescopes however, had reached the technological level required for parallax detection and astronomers were caught up in a tantalising race to reach this holy grail of astronomy.

Even so, for reasons that are still not entirely clear, Henderson apparently saw no urgency in further analysing his observations of alpha Centauri and instead applied himself to more routine tasks after returning to his native country. Had he possessed the confidence to formally publish his results, his claim to fame would have been much greater. The announcement from the German astronomer *Friedrich Wilhelm Bessel* that he had managed to measure the parallax and therefore the distance of another star, *61 Cyg*, finally motivated Henderson to analyse his results in more detail in late 1838. In January 1839, more than six years after his observations had been made, he published his results which were read at a meeting of the Royal Astronomical Society (RAS). His initial parallax estimations determined the distance of alpha Centauri to be at 3.25 light years (one light year being the distance travelled by light in a vacuum in one year) when in fact it is 4.37 light years. He later improved his estimate to 3.57 light years, after obtaining better quality results from his successor (and good friend) at Cape Town, astronomer *Thomas Maclear*.

Although the accuracy of the results may not be great by modern standards, Henderson had gauged the distance of a star, a feat of historical significance. Incredibly, he had achieved this without fully believing or realising it himself, and so came second to formally publishing a result. It is because of this that it was Bessel and not Henderson who was awarded the Gold Medal from the RAS and who is generally acknowledged as the winner of the scientific race. In fact within just a few months, *three* astronomers had published their star parallax results (the third one being the German-Russian astronomer *Friedrich Georg Wilhelm von Struve*). So important was the feat that when *John Herschel*, the president of the RAS, awarded the medal, he declared: *"Gentlemen, I congratulate you and myself that we have lived to see the great and hitherto impassable barrier to our excursions into the sidereal universe—that barrier against which we have chafed so long and so vainly – almost simultaneously overleaped at three different points. It is the greatest and most glorious triumph which practical astronomy has ever witnessed"*.

Thomas Henderson Commemoration Plaque

So how is this fascinating story of science history connected to Calton Hill? After returning to Scotland Henderson was appointed the first ever

Scottish Astronomer Royal and Professor of Astronomy at Edinburgh university. He worked at the Calton Hill observatory for ten years, recording over 60,000 observations of star positions. He was elected a fellow of the Royal Astronomical Society in 1832, the Royal Society of Edinburgh in 1834, and the Royal Society of London in 1840. Henderson died from heart disease at his home, in 1844. Two years before his death he met Bessel in Edinburgh in what he described as one of the highlights of his life. A plaque outside the main observatory building commemorates him and the house in which he spent his final years is also signposted at the foot of the hill. Although little known and difficult to imagine, a scientific quest which started in antiquity, was concluded in this very part of the city of Edinburgh.

Thomas Henderson's House

Henderson's successor as Scottish Astronomer Royal may not have been the first to measure the distance to a star but was a pioneering scientist and although never formally attended university, was probably one of the most colourful scientific characters of his time. His name was *Charles Piazzi Smyth* and he was born in Naples, in Italy, in 1819, the son of an Admiral. He was given the middle name Piazzi after his godfather, the Italian astronomer *Giuseppe Piazzi*. On returning to Britain, the family settled in Bedford, where his father built an observatory and Piazzi Smyth started to learn astronomy. He became an assistant to Thomas Maclear (Henderson's successor at the Cape of Good Hope), when he was just 16. In 1845, at the age of just 26, he was appointed Astronomer Royal for Scotland at the Calton Hill observatory and also Professor of Astronomy at the University of Edinburgh.

Portrait of Charles Piazzi Smyth

Frustrated by the poor conditions for observation at Calton Hill, Smyth together with his wife (a geologist who was also his faithful scientific partner), travelled around Europe undertaking scientific work. Their expedition to the peaks of Tenerife in the Canary Islands (which actually coincided with their honeymoon), produced impressive results. Smyth was the first astronomer to realise that positioning telescopes on mountain tops significantly improved observations. In fact, the Teide Observatory on the Teide peak of the Canary Islands that the Smyths had visited on their honeymoon, became one of the first international observatories in 1964.

Smyth pioneered work in spectrometry and photography and was interested in weather forecasting and painting. His popular account of his voyage to Tenerife, was also the first book ever illustrated by stereoscopic photographs (3D photographs). For his works he was awarded the Keith gold medal by the Royal Society of Edinburgh.

Unfortunately, however, he also became increasingly eccentric and alienated from his colleagues. In 1888 he resigned as Astronomer Royal for Scotland in protest to the underfunding of the Calton Hill Observatory (which was subsequently moved to Blackford Hill, in 1896). Before retiring he resided at the foot of Calton Hill, at 15 Royal Terrace. Smyth also unprecedentedly resigned from the Royal Society of London, in 1874, for which he had been elected fellow in 1857, after some disagreement regarding the publication of his work. He left Edinburgh and spent his final years in Yorkshire, where he died in 1900.

One of the main reasons Smyth drew criticism from the scientific community was his involvement in the study and measurement of the Great Pyramid of Giza in Egypt. Although his surveying of the Great Pyramid was the most accurate to date and his use of flash photography on the field truly groundbreaking, he also developed some dubious theories, including the claim that the mathematical structure of the pyramid encoded the events of the Old Testament. His book, "Our Inheritance in the Great Pyramid" first published in 1864 drew a large cult following (to an extent still thriving to this day), but his far fetched claims seriously damaged his scientific reputation. His grave at Ripon Yorkshire is marked by a small stone pyramid topped by a Christian cross. The crater Piazzi Smyth on the moon is named after him.

Site:

The first observatory on Calton Hill was founded in 1776 by *Thomas Short*, an optician from Leith (the port of Edinburgh) whose brother was a telescope maker in London , to a design by *James Craig*, the architect of Edinburgh's New Town. The original building is now called the *Observatory House* and still stands in the observatory complex.

Observatory House (Old Observatory)

The nearby *Transit House*, dating from 1812, was used for accurate timekeeping by astronomical observation until the time of Thomas Henderson.

Transit House

The *New Observatory* (as it was called) was founded in 1818, to the plan of *William Playfair*, a famous architect of the time, who also designed many of the other neoclassical monuments on the hill. It has a central observatory dome on an octagonal drum and its design is inspired from the observatory designed and used by the famous Danish astronomer *Tycho Brache* in the 16th century and the Tower of the Winds in Athens. It obtained royal status and was renamed the Royal Observatory after a visit from King George IV in 1822.

New Observatory

The Observatory was handed over to the Town Council and became the *City Observatory* at the end of the 19th century. Unfortunately, it spent most of the past century deteriorating, although it was used by the Astronomical Society of Edinburgh from the late 1930s until 2009. Fortunately, in recent years, a small, not-for-profit visual arts organisation, the *Collective Gallery* has helped restore the complex buildings giving them new life by turning them into a space for contemporary art exhibitions. The main dome can now be visited admission free (although donations are happily accepted) and houses two of the 19th century telescopes which can both be viewed.

Special note should be made of the *Nelson Monument* (the British admiral who led his fleet to victory at Trafalgar in 1805) which looks like an upturned telescope erected close to the main observatory buildings. In the 19th century time keeping was an important duty of the Royal Observatory. A telescope was used to regulate a clock, from which the citizens of Edinburgh and mariners could synchronise their own clocks. In 1854, a time ball was erected on top of the Nelson Monument by Charles Piazzi Smyth, in full view of the harbour, to save mariners the trip to the top of the hill. The time ball's mechanism was connected by an underground wire to a time clock in the Observatory. Just before 1 pm, the ball would be raised, and then exactly on the hour a signal was sent electrically via the wire, causing the ball to drop. In 1861 the "one o'clock gun" was installed at Edinburgh Castle to also provide an audible time signal. The gun's clock was connected to the clock on Calton hill by a 4,020-foot overhead wire. The time ball is no longer triggered automatically but manually (every day except Sundays, weather permitting) by an operator at the same time as the gun at the Castle goes off; so if you do visit, try and be there at the right moment.

Nelson Monument

Finally, an interesting twist in the history of the observatory concerns a woman named *Maria Short*, who arrived from the West Indies in

1827 claiming to be the daughter of Thomas Short who built the first observatory building. Maria's claim (though never proven) made her the rightful owner of Thomas's telescope which she used to set up her own observatory (next to the one designed by Playfair), in 1835. What's more, it also included a *Camera Obscura,* used to project a "virtual" tour of the city for visitors (a kind of predecessor to the modern cinema), an attraction which was to fascinate Edinburgh visitors for years to come.

Eventually, under pressure from the council Maria was evicted from Calton Hill and, in 1853, she relocated her business – by then called *Short's Observatory* – to the Royal Mile. The attraction has since been expanded and named "Camera Obscura and World of Illusions" (see, https://www.camera-obscura.co.uk).

Where to find it:

The **Calton Hill Observatory** overlooks the eastern end of Princess Street (Edinburgh's main shopping street) and is easily reached from the city centre.

Where to digest your knowledge:

For the most authentic astronomical experience on Calton Hill, grab a coffee and a snack from the **Kiosk by Gardener's Cottage** situated at the east entrance of the Observatory. Choose one of the numerous benches scattered around and enjoy the views that Robert Louis Stevenson raved about.

- **Address:** 38 Calton Hill, Edinburgh EH7 5AA
- **Website:** https://www.collective-edinburgh.art/restaurant

Did you know?

The original clock at the Observatory was called a "Politician's Clock" as it presented two faces: One face pointed inwards, to be read by the astronomers, the other pointed outwards, for the ordinary citizens and mariners to set their watches and clocks accurately. Though the Politician's Clock can no longer be used to set your watch by (it was struck by lightning in the 1860s) you can still view it through the window of the Transit House much in the same way as you would have done 200 years ago.

Royal Observatory Blackford Hill

Background:

In 1896, the **Royal Observatory** moved from Calton Hill to a site at **Blackford Hill** in Edinburgh's south side. A reason for choosing this position was that the prevailing wind direction is from the south, thus blowing smoke from the city away from the Observatory. The government agreed to build and maintain a new Royal Observatory after *James Ludovic Lindsay*, 26th Earl of Crawford, a distinguished amateur astronomer himself, gifted to the nation the instruments from his own observatory in Aberdeenshire; he also donated his unique library of astronomy books.

In the 20th century the Royal Observatory gained a world wide reputation and currently houses establishments that include a university astronomy research group (active in several international research collaborations), the UK Astronomy Technology Centre (which designs instruments for use on several major telescopes around the world) and a Visitor Centre. Its library (including the world famous *Crawford Collection* gifted by the Earl of Crawford in 1888), contains one of the most extensive and valuable astronomical collections in the world. Finally, the Archives of the Royal Observatory consist of correspondence, scientific and administrative papers of the former Astronomical Institution of Edinburgh, the Astronomers Royal for Scotland, and the Earl of Crawford, and also photographs, sketchbooks and diaries of Charles Piazzi Smyth.

Royal Observatory at Blackford Hill

Site:

The views from Blackford Hill are stunning and it is worth visiting the site even just for this. For those wanting a more scientific experience, the Visitor Centre runs a variety of outreach programmes and events for the public. Public Astronomy Evenings can be booked (online or by phone) for selected Friday evenings, and include a tour of the beautiful Victorian telescope dome, observing outside on the flat roof (weather permitting), information about the science and engineering projects conducted today at the Royal Observatory Edinburgh, and a question time. During the winter time, astronomy talks are given on selected Mondays that also require booking in advance. The presentations cover a variety of astronomy topics and often include advice to beginners for navigating the night sky and a roundup of recent astronomical news.

Where to find it:

- **Address:** Blackford Hill, Edinburgh EH9 3HJ
- **Phone:** +44 (0) 131 6688404
- **Website:** https://www.roe.ac.uk

Where to digest your knowledge:

Although a 20 minute bus ride from Blackford Hill, the **Southern Cross** cafe on Cockburn street, has a truly astronomical name (the Southern Cross is one of the most famous star constellations), and is worth visiting on your return to the city centre.

- **Address:** 63A Cockburn St, Edinburgh EH1 1BU
- **Website:** https://www.facebook.com/scrosscafe

Did you know?

The Crawford Collection contains approximately 15,000 items dating back to the 13th century including some that are extremely rare. Viewing is possible by prior request.

Salisbury Crags

Background:

Edinburgh's volcanic past is evident when you look towards the imposing hills of Arthur's Seat and **Salisbury Crags**. The former was formed by an extinct volcano system around 340 million years ago, whereas the Crags, situated in Holyrood Park, are a single sheet of tough dolerite rock which is about 325 million years old. The dolerite rock was formed by the process of magma intrusion deep underground; magma rose to this level, then spread out horizontally, forcing its way between layers of existing rock.

Salisbury Crags as Viewed from Calton Hill

It is this unique landscape that inspired the farmer and naturalist *James Hutton* in the 18th century to contrive one of the most important theories of his time. Hutton was the first to realise that the Earth is continually being formed by geological processes over millions of years and is thus justifiably referred to as the "father of modern geology". He was one of the key figures of the *Scottish Enlightenment*, a period covering the 18th and early 19th centuries which was characterised by an outpouring of new intellectual and scientific ideas; Edinburgh in particular was regarded as "a hotbed of genius".

Portrait of James Hutton

James Hutton was born in Edinburgh in 1726. Although initially entering the legal profession, he was more interested in chemistry and ended up studying medicine (the closest field to chemistry at the time), at Edinburgh University, then in Paris and Leiden, graduating in 1749. In 1750 he returned to Edinburgh and together with his friend *James Davie*, ran a profitable partnership on the production of sal ammoniac from soot. This proved very important, as the profits made by Hutton enabled him to move to a family farm he had inherited in Berwickshire (in southwestern Scotland) where he lived for 14 years. It was his farming experience that fuelled his interest in the way the land changes and interacts with the forces of nature thus paving the way for his geological theories.

Once becoming interested in the geological processes, Hutton travelled extensively with the aim of studying and observing different rocks. He was intrigued by his findings, which included that of fossilised shells high above sea level. In his travels he also observed that most rocks are the consolidated products of destruction of still older rocks and later in life concluded that: *"We are thus led to see a circulation in the matter of this globe, and a beautiful economy in the works of nature. This earth, like the body of an animal, is wasted at the same time that it is repaired. It has a state of growth and augmentation; it has another state, which is that of diminution and decay. This world is thus destroyed in one part, but it is renewed in another; and the operations by which this world is thus constantly renewed, are as evident to the scientific eye, as are those in which it is necessarily destroyed"*.

Hutton left his farm and moved back to Edinburgh around 1768, where he spent time strolling in the Meadows (the still popular public park) with his friends *Adam Smith* (the world - famous economist, philosopher) and *Joseph Black* (the chemist who discovered carbon dioxide and latent heat). The three of them also founded the "Oyster Club", a weekly dining club that hosted many notable scientists and philosophers who exchanged their exciting ideas. The former site of the club is currently a popular bar and music venue and is situated at 8-12 Niddry Street South.

Site of the Oyster Club

Of all the new ideas circulating at the time, Hutton's so called "*unifor-mitarian*" theory of geology was one of the most groundbreaking. The main concept was that the centre of the Earth is a massive heat source, where continuous processes destroy and reform rocks. A startling consequence of this theory was that the Earth was millions of years old. As his fellow traveller *John Playfair* later recorded, "the mind seem to grow giddy by looking so far into the abyss of time". This idea of *deep time* directly contradicted the contemporary belief that our planet had been created only about 6,000 years ago as described by the biblical book of Genesis. Many of his fellow scientists openly disagreed with Hutton as they believed that changes in geology happened as a result of natural disasters such as volcanic eruptions or floods.

Hutton's findings were presented to the newly formed Royal Society of Edinburgh (he was one of the founding members), in 1785. In 1788 he published two papers in the *Transactions of the Royal Society of Edinburgh* that are nowadays considered the turning point after which geology became a science founded upon the principle of uniformitarianism. Hutton further detailed his views by publishing his *Theory of the Earth*, in 1795. He died two years later and is buried opposite the vault of his friend Joseph Black, in Greyfriars Kirkyard. Hutton never married, although at the age 21 he fathered a son, James Smeaton Hutton. He provided his son and his son's mother with financial assistance but chose to have little contact with them. In fact, it has been postulated that Hutton delayed his return to Edinburgh until the summer of 1750 because of this.

Hutton's close friend, the mathematician and scientist *John Playfair* (the uncle of *William Playfair* who designed the Calton Hill Observatory), with whom he had been on a geological trip in 1788, summarised his work and published it in 1802 under the title "*Illustrations of the Huttonian Theory of the Earth*". Playfair's publication helped to disseminate Hutton's ideas thus enhancing their influence on the development of geology.

The site:

A hike up Arthur's seat and the adjacent Salisbury Crags is a must for anyone visiting Edinburgh. Apart from offering stunning views of the city, the landscape itself is beautiful. For anyone fascinated by Hutton's achievements there is a particular section of the Crags that will be of special interest. It is where he found proof of his theory that igneous rocks were crystallised from magma and so is appropriately named "Hutton's Section". A plaque can be found on the spot, providing further information. Note that the footpath leading to this is sometimes closed off for safety reasons due to the presence of loose rocks.

Hutton's Section

Hutton lived most of his years after returning to Edinburgh at a house just off the Pleasance in the south side of the city. Not surprisingly, it had a view of the Salisbury Crags providing the great scientist with the inspiration he needed. The house has long been demolished but a memorial garden can now be found where it once stood and is well worth a visit. Stones have been placed taken from different locations important to the development of Hutton's theories. Hutton's belief in deep geological time is encapsulated in his phrase *"we find no vestige of a beginning, no prospect of an end"*, which is inscribed on a plaque also placed at the site.

James Hutton Memorial Garden

Where to find it:

The **Salisbury Crags** are located in Holyrood Park whereas the John Hutton Memorial Garden is at 10, Viewcraig Gardens.

Where to digest your knowledge:

Edinburgh is known as "The Athens of the North", so a visit to a Greek bistro seems appropriate. A few minutes' walk from the northwestern entrance to the Meadows (where James Hutton used to go out for a stroll with his distinguished friends), try **Taxidi Greek Bistro** for excellent coffee and some of the most authentic Greek food outside Greece.
  · **Address:** 6 Brougham St, Edinburgh EH3 9JH
  · **Website: https://www.facebook.com/Taxidi-107882179904212/**

Did you know?

One of James Hutton's famous geological trips was conducted with *George Maxwell-Clerk*, the great grandfather of James Clerk Maxwell, the famous physicist.

Dynamic Earth

Background:

Dynamic Earth is a visitor attraction that aims is to improve the understanding of the processes that have shaped the Earth in an interactive fun way both for adults and kids and is appropriately situated very close to where James Hutton, the father of geology, lived for most of his life. The so called *Deep Time Machine* is used to time travel to the origins of the universe and it is also possible to feel the tremors of an earthquake or a volcanic eruption, explore a prehistoric glacier and meet up with a dinosaur. A particular highlight is the ShowDome Cinema with its 360 degree digital dome technology and thunderous surround sound, the only one of its kind in Scotland.

A wide range of learning experiences are offered which include over 35 different curriculum linked workshops, an outdoor learning program, a dedicated community learning program, a regular kids club as well as holiday activity programs and one off events throughout the year.

Site:

The centre opened in 1999 as part of an urban regeneration plan for former industrial land at the lower end of Holyrood Road. It has a spectacular setting, next to the Scottish Parliament building and at the foot of Salisbury Crags. The building's structure consists of a steel mast-supported membrane stretched over a steel skeleton.

Dynamic Earth

Where to find it:

- **Address:** Holyrood Rd, Edinburgh EH8 8AS
- **Phone:** +44 (0) 131 5507800
- **Website:** https://www.dynamicearth.co.uk

Where to digest your knowledge:

Hemma ("at home", in Swedish) is one of a string of Edinburgh cafes and bars with a Swedish theme. Having a family friendly atmosphere, it is the ideal place to relax after spending a few hours at the Dynamic Earth.

- **Address:** 73 Holyrood Rd, Edinburgh EH8 8AU

· **Website:** https://www.bodabar.com/hemma

Did you know?

The design of the Dynamic Earth incorporates the original wall that formed the outer perimeter of a brewery site.

National Museum of Scotland

Background:

The **National Museum of Scotland** caters for a diverse set of interests. It covers themes such as the history of the Scottish nation, our world cultural heritage, the decorative arts and wonders of the natural world. Visiting it you will come across meteorites, dinosaurs, giant whales, and even a grand Millennium clock that swings into action on the hour every hour. You will also learn about famous Scots whose ideas and inventions shaped the modern world.

The *Science and Technology* galleries in particular, feature highlights such as the Nobel medal awarded to the Edinburgh University Emeritus Professor *Peter Higgs* (who famously predicted the existence of a subatomic particle which was subsequently found experimentally in 2012), replicas of the first telephone devices invented by the famous Scottish inventor *Alexander Graham Bell* in the late 19th century, and the stuffed remains of *Dolly the sheep*, the first mammal cloned from an adult somatic (body) cell. A host of other inventions and innovations are also brought to life through displays and interactive exhibits and are organised as follows:

Communications, transport, industry, engineering, energy and medicine: Revealing how scientific and technological inventions have affected our lives with particular emphasis on the rich history of innovation in Scotland.

Explore: Family oriented activities bringing science to life with hands-on games and interactive exhibits.

Making It: Investigating how manufacturing and engineering have changed our way of life.

Communicate: Describing the evolution of telecommunications, from semaphore to smart phones.

Technology by Design: Celebrating scientific discoveries from the first computers to Edinburgh's key role in the history of prosthetics.

Enquire: Exploring how scientists have sought to answer fundamental questions such as those posed by Professor Higgs.

Energise: Focusing on the sources, generation and uses of energy.

The National Museum of Scotland also hosts events related to the *Edinburgh Science Festival* that takes place once a year (see, https://www.sciencefestival.co.uk).

Site:

The National Museum of Scotland was formed in 2006 with the merger of the new Museum of Scotland and the adjacent Royal Museum. The two connected buildings retain distinctive characters: the Museum of Scotland is housed in a modern building opened in 1998, while the former Royal Museum building was begun in 1861, and partially opened in 1866, with a Victorian Venetian Renaissance facade and a grand central hall that provides a spectacular start to a museum visit. The building housing the former Royal museum underwent a major refurbishment and reopened in 2011.

Also worth checking out on a sunny day, on the outside wall of the museum, is a unique modern sundial (that tells the time of day from the position of the shadow of the Sun). Finally, not to be missed is the roof terrace with amazing views of Edinburgh and its surroundings.

National Museum of Scotland

Where to find it:

The museum is part of the National Museums of Scotland and is free to visit at:

- **Address:** Chambers St, Edinburgh EH1 1JF
- **Phone:** +44 (0) 300 123 6789
- **Website:** https://www.nms.ac.uk

Free guided tours are also offered on a first come first served basis.

Where to digest your knowledge:

After wandering through the natural world galleries of the national Museum, visiting the **Zebra Coffee Company** may sound tempting. Tucked away conveniently just off the Royal Mile, it is an ideal escape from the hustle and bustle of Edinburgh's busiest and most touristic area.

- **Address:** 16 Bank St, Edinburgh EH1 2LN
- **Website:** http://zebracoffeeco.co.uk

Did you know?

If you are interested in aircraft and flight in general, the **National Museum of Flight** (see, https://www.nms.ac.uk) is also part of the National Museums of Scotland. It is one home to one of the best aircraft collections in Europe and can be reached in 40 minutes from Edinburgh by car.

Merchiston Tower

Background:

The word *logarithm* probably brings a shiver to those not particularly keen on mathematics but who had to endure learning it at school. Nevertheless, the use of this mathematical tool actually simplifies many calculations, particularly those involving the multiplication and division of very small or very large numbers. Also, when measuring a quantity that can vary from being very small to very large, such as the power of an earthquake, it is more convenient to use a *logarithmic* scale rather than a *linear* (conventional) one. In simple words this means that an earthquake measuring 6 on the *Richter* scale (used to measure earthquakes) will be 10 times larger than one measuring 5 and 100 times larger than an earthquake measuring 4. Each increase of one unit on this logarithmic scale is equivalent to a tenfold increase in the actual earthquake power. As earthquakes can vary from being almost negligible to those having a devastating effect, this is a convenient method of quantifying them.

The person who is credited with discovering logarithms was born in **Merchiston Tower**, a castle on the outskirts of Edinburgh, in 1550, and his name is *John Napier*. His ingenious method of calculation facilitated the solution of laborious arithmetical problems and for this reason he came to be respected by many famous scientists. Adaptations of Napier's work such as the "slide rule", were used right up to the 1970s when electronic calculators were introduced.

Portrait of John Napier

John Napier was born into a wealthy and privileged family. His father was *Sir Archibald Napier* of Merchiston Castle, and his mother was *Janet Bothwell*, daughter of the politician and judge *Francis Bothwell*, Lord of Session, and a sister of *Adam Bothwell* who became the Bishop of

Orkney. At the age of 13 he was sent to St Andrews University but on the advice of his uncle, the Bishop of Orkney, soon left to study in Europe.

When he returned to Scotland in 1571 he married and went to live at Gartness in Stirlingshire, spending much of his time on self study. Napier kept to himself for long periods and wore long dark cloaks and skull caps. It was also said that he would carry a black spider in a small box, and that his favourite pet was a black rooster. His unconventional ways attracted the attention of local people and he soon acquired the reputation of possessing magical abilities. This was not the best reputation to acquire in medieval Europe and he was probably quite lucky not to be formally accused of witchcraft, a charge that could have led to the death penalty.

His pet rooster is also the focus of an amusing story as it was apparently used to trap a thief in the household. Napier informed his servants that the bird could tell the difference between an honest and a dishonest person and would crow if a thief stroked it. He then covered his pet in soot, tied it up in a dark room and instructed every one of his servants to stroke it. The thief was soon found out, as for fear of being identified, he did not go near the rooster walking out the room with clean albeit guilty hands.

Apart from mathematics and strange pets, Napier was also interested in theological issues and was fiercely opposed to the Catholic Church. In fact, ironically, it was his theological work, and in particular his publication entitled "*A plaine discovery of the whole Revelation of St John*", that made him famous before his mathematical achievements did.

His first wife, Elizabeth, died in 1579 and he subsequently married Agnes Chisholm with whom he brought up a large family. When his father died in 1608, Napier and his family moved back to Merchiston Tower, where he lived for the remainder of his life.

In 1614 Napier published his most famous work entitled "*Mirifici logarithmorum canonis descriptio*" ("*Description of the Marvelous Canon of Logarithms*"). Amongst those impressed by the work was the English mathematician Henry Briggs, who visited Napier the following year and subsequently produced a revised table of logarithms further simplifying calculations. This opened the way to important scientific advances particularly in the field of astronomy. For example, the famous German astronomer *Johannes Kepler* first studied Napier's work in 1617 and himself developed mathematical methods based on algorithms. Kepler's scientific work eventually led to the discovery of his laws describing the motion of planets around the sun. Such was the respect that the great astronomer had for Napier that he actually dedicated one of his books to him.

Alongside his theoretical contributions to mathematics (which also included popularising the use of the decimal point), Napier invented several devices to use as calculators, the best known of which consists of an assortment of rods known as "Napier's Bones". The name of this invention derives from the earliest versions that were made of ivory and resembled skeletal fingers. "Napier's Bones" could be used to perform complex calculations without advanced mathematical knowledge and thus became extremely popular. A set can be viewed at the National Museum of Scotland.

Finally, to counter the threat of invasion by the Spanish Armada, Napier produced designs for several weapons of war such as a set of mirrors that would use the reflecting sunlight to destroy enemy ships. The Spanish ships never actually attacked Britain so Napier's designs were not put into practice.

John Napier died at the age of 67 and (although this is not certain) he is believed to be buried in Saint Cuthbert's Churchyard at the western end of Princess street. A memorial plaque (in Latin) can be found inside the church.

Napier Memorial Plaque

The site:

Merchiston Tower, also known as *Merchiston Castle*, was probably built by *Alexander Napier*, the second Laird of Merchiston, around 1454. During John Napier's time Scotland was engulfed in a civil war between supporters of the abdicated Mary Queen of Scots and those loyal to her son King James VI. The strategic position of Merchiston castle meant that it was frequently under siege. Troops loyal to the infant King James VI were garrisoned there to prevent supplies reaching the Queen's supporters in the city of Edinburgh. As a result, during this time, the Tower suffered extensive damage.

Nowadays the restored Merchiston Tower is part of the Merchiston campus of Edinburgh Napier University, housing a bust of the man himself and a set of "Napier's Bones".

Merchiston Tower

Where to find it:

Merchiston Tower is located at 10, Colinton Road, in the Merchiston area. You can view it from the outside during university opening times. Official visits can be made by appointment only through the university.

Where to digest your knowledge:

Very close to Merchiston Tower you can find the family run, French themed, **Mugs** cafe. The selection of cakes offered is such, that deciding which one to choose, would probably have inspired Napier to invent another mathematical method!
- **Address:** 26 Morningside Rd, Edinburgh EH10 4DA
- **Website (on tripadvisor):** https://www.tripadvisor.co.uk

Did you know?

Apart from *Napier University*, John Napier also has an electrical engineering unit and a lunar crater named after him, both called "Neper".

George Square

Background:

George Square, the most prominent square in the city of Glasgow, will impress any visitor with its grand architecture. The imposing City Chambers building for example, which opened in 1888, is considered one of the most beautiful civic buildings in the UK and is a major tourist attraction.

Within the square itself there are also several statues including those of a famous engineer and of a brilliant experimental chemist. In the southwestern corner sits the statue of *James Watt* (1736-1819), after whom the unit of power is named. Every bulb in your house comes with an indication of the number of Watts it consumes (for example 60 W). While working as an instrument maker at the University of Glasgow, Watt became interested in steam engines and eventually built the first practical one in 1776. Watt's design saved significantly more fuel compared to earlier designs, radically improving efficiency and power output. His innovation is now considered one of the driving forces of the industrial revolution.

James Watt Statue

At the southeastern corner of the square you can find the statue of *Thomas Graham* (1805–1869) a chemist who studied the behaviour of gasses (formulating a law now named after him) and who also pioneered the technique of "dialysis" which is used for the treatment of kidney disease.

Thomas Graham Statue

The statues of the famous pioneers are easily identified, but if you look carefully enough you can also seek out a series of science related inscriptions that probably escape the attention of most visitors. Physical units are important in science but also in everyday activities such as farming and trading. In the 18th and 19th centuries, in order to ensure the fair exchange of goods, strict measurement standards were publicly displayed. For example, to obtain a consistent measurement of length, a standard inch would be marked for everyone to check against.

There are three sets of measurement standards to be found in George Square. On the exterior wall of the City Chambers, the standard inch, foot, two-feet and imperial yard measurements are mounted.

Standard Measurements Outside City Chambers

The less familiar nowadays, standard *chain* measure, is located at the east side of north lawn. The chain is a unit of length equal to 22 yards (just over 20 meters). It is subdivided into 100 *links* or 4 *rods*. There are also 10 chains in a *furlong*, and 80 chains in one *statute mile*. Many of the physical units used in the past were derived from farming. So for example, the furlong (meaning furrow length) was the distance an ox could plough without resting, and an *acre* (still used today), the area that could be ploughed in one day with a yoke of oxen pulling a wooden plough. An acre is one furlong long and one chain wide.

Part of the Standard Chain

Finally, close by you can also find a 100 foot measure, as seen below.

Part of the 100 ft Standard Measurement

The site:

George Square was opened in 1787 and was named in honour of King George III. It has often been the scene of political gatherings, concerts, riots and protests.

Where to find it:

George Square is in the heart of Glasgow's city centre. After your scientific walk there, it is recommended you go for a stroll on the adjacent *Buchanan* street, Glasgow's bustling pedestrian area.

Where to digest your knowledge:

Princes Square shopping centre, the conversion of a 19th century cobbled courtyard off Buchanan Street, has in the past been voted the "building of the century" for Scotland. There are several boutique shops, restaurants and cafes inside the building, the **Tinderbox Espresso Bar** being one of best places on the terrace to enjoy a coffee while admiring the beautiful surroundings.

- **Address:** 48 Buchanan St, Glasgow G1 3JN
- **Website:** https://www.princessquare.co.uk/food-drink/cafes/tinderbox/

Did you know?

Prior to being legally replaced by the English measurement system, the traditional Scots measurement units were used in Scotland. An example is the "Scottish ell", a unit of length equivalent to approximately 94 cm. The Scottish mile was also longer than the English one, and a reference to this is made in *Tam o' Shanter*, the famous poem written by Scotland's national poet, *Robert Burns*. In the first verse Burns tells us that: "*While we sit bousing at the nappy, And getting fou and unco happy, We think na on the lang Scots miles*".

Lord Kelvin at the University of Glasgow

Background:

If Edinburgh has James Clerk Maxwell, then Glasgow has William Thomson, more commonly known as **Lord Kelvin**. Although born in Belfast (in 1824), he came to Glasgow at a young age (his father James was Professor of mathematics at the University of Glasgow) and went on to become the city's most famous scientist, a real celebrity of his time.

When visiting the university area, you could be excused for thinking that everything around it is named after the great man: Kelvingrove, Kelvindside, Kelvinhall, all seem to derive from him. In fact, it is actually the other way around, as it is the great physicist who took the title *Baron Kelvin of Largs* (becoming the first ever science peer in 1892), from the river Kelvin that flows at the foot of the University of Glasgow's beautiful campus, and the coastal town of *Largs* where he spent much of his time in his latter years.

Portrait of Lord Kelvin

Kelvin attended university classes at the University of Glasgow from the age of 10 setting the record for the youngest student and wrote his first scientific paper when he was only 16. His interest in physics was such that immediately after retiring, at the age of 75, he also matriculated as the university's oldest student.

Kelvin did not actually formally graduate from University of Glasgow, instead from 1841 to 1845 he attended Cambridge University, graduated as Second Wrangler, won the First Smith's Prize and had one of his examiners declare to another that "you and I are just about fit to mend his pens". He subsequently spent time at a Paris laboratory and in 1846, at the remarkably young age of 22, was appointed to the chair of natural philosophy at the University of Glasgow. He remained in this position for an astonishing number of 53 years, refusing offers from some of the most important scientific establishments of the time, including the Cavendish Laboratory established under Maxwell. Kelvin married twice (his first wife Margaret passed away in 1870) but had no children.

While a professor he taught some 7,000 students from all over the world, established an advanced class in mathematical physics and the first physics laboratory in Britain. He also co-authored the text book "Treatise on Natural Philosophy" with physicist *Peter Guthrie Tait* in 1867, considered one of the most important scientific textbooks ever written.

It is for his scientific research, however, that Lord Kelvin is mainly remembered, having published more than 600 scientific papers on a variety of topics. He famously proposed an absolute scale of temperature now known as the *Kelvin Scale* (zero degrees Kelvin is the lowest attainable temperature equivalent to -273.15 degrees Celcius). In 1851 he presented to the Royal Society of Edinburgh a paper on the dynamical theory of heat containing a statement of the second law of thermodynamics which, in simple words, asserts that heat always flows from a hotter to a colder object. In 1856 he also published work on electricity and magnetism which subsequently inspired Maxwell to develop his remarkable new theory of electromagnetism (a theory which Kelvin himself actually never accepted).

Kelvin was equally famous for his practical inventions, some of which also helped him become very wealthy. He was a scientific adviser in the laying of the Atlantic telegraph cables in the 1850s and 1860s, for which he was knighted in 1866. With a great interest in nautical engineering he also developed an extremely accurate compass, a tide measuring instrument and depth measuring equipment. He invented many electrical instruments and his house in Glasgow was the first to be lit by electric light.

Ironically, the scientist who laid the cornerstones for some of the most important scientific theories and who was also a prolific inventor of new technologies, at the end of his life came to be seen by some scientific circles as a reactionary unable to anticipate the dawn of modern physics in the way those like Maxwell did. He doubted the existence of atoms and did not fully accept the theory of radioactivity. He also believed that the origin of life was a matter better left to theologians, and so opposed the doctrines of evolution as proposed by *Charles Darwin* arguing that the Earth and the Sun could not be more than 100 million years old (when we now know them to be about 4.5 billion years old). Despite this, when he died in 1907, he received the ultimate honour as he was buried in Westminster Abbey alongside *Isaac Newton* and to this day is regarded as one of the greatest intellectual giants of the 19th century.

The site:

Evidence of Lord Kelvin's time at the University of Glasgow can be found around the campus but the real highlight is the permanent display entitled "Lord Kelvin: Revolutionary Scientist", at the university's *Hunterian Museum* (admission free). This is a world-famous collection of historical items and original scientific instruments located on the balcony level of the museum's main hall. Portraits of the man can also be found at the nearby *Hunterian Art Gallery*.

Also close to the museum, at No.11, the Square, is the house where Kelvin lived from 1870 until his retirement in 1899. Probably the first house in the world to be lit entirely by electricity it still houses a clock of Kelvin's own design.

Kelvin's House

Moving to the south side of the main building, you can also admire what is known as "Kelvin's sundial". Sundials use the shadow of the sun to measure time and this impressive globe has no fewer than five of them incorporated on it. The globe is believed to have been designed either by Kelvin himself or by his father.

Kelvin's Sundial

Finally, one of the most beautiful Glasgow parks, lying just east of the university campus, is *Kelvingrove* park, where a statue of the great physicist can be admired.

Kelvin's Statue at Kelvingrove Park

Where to find it:

The University of Glasgow campus is truly beautiful and is situated in the West End of the city, accessed from the Hillhead tube station.

Where to digest your knowledge:

Dean's Deli Coffee is a cosy little independent coffee shop, minutes' away from where Lord Kelvin used to live and teach. It serves good coffee, cakes and light snacks.
- **Address:** 23 Byres Rd, Glasgow G11 5RD
- **Website:** https://deansdelicoffee.co.uk

Did you know?

Although he is buried in Westminster Abbey, a memorial stone to Lord Kelvin can also be found in the Glasgow necropolis, the Victorian cemetery at the East End of the city.

Glasgow Science Centre

Background:

The **Glasgow Science Centre** is a visitor attraction that was opened in 2001 and is composed of three principal buildings: the Science Mall, Glasgow Tower and an IMAX cinema.

Glasgow Science Centre

The Science Mall which is particularly attractive to those interested in science, is a crescent shape structure representing the canted hull of a ship, a reference to the adjacent "canting basin", where vessels were brought to have the marine growth removed from their hulls. It comprises of three floors containing more than 250 science-themed exhibits. Highlights include a Science Show Theatre, a state of the art Planetarium, the Space Zone with interesting facts on our solar system, the "My World of Work Live" interactive exhibition space where visitors can explore opportunities in science related careers, an interactive exhibition about human health called "BodyWorks", and an area designed for young children, the "Big Explorer".

The Glasgow Tower offers stunning views of Glasgow (although often closed due to high winds) and the IMAX cinema has the largest screen of its kind in Scotland, showing 3D films that are often science inspired.

Site:

The Glasgow Science Centre is located on the south bank of the River Clyde and is part of the Clyde Waterfront Regeneration area. If you have the time, take a walk along the bank, the waterfront path can lead you right to the heart of Glasgow's city centre. The Glasgow Science Centre also hosts events related to the *Glasgow Science Festival* that takes place once a year (see, http://www.glasgowsciencefestival.org.uk).

Where to find it:

- **Address:** 50 Pacific Quay, Glasgow G51 1EA
- **Phone:** +44 (0) 141 4205000
- **Website:** https://www.glasgowsciencecentre.org

Where to digest your knowledge:

The hip *Finnieston* neighbourhood is only a 15 minutes' walk across the river and is full of trendy cafes and restaurants. One of the best is the **Steamie Coffee Roasters**, with a friendly and relaxed atmosphere serving excellent coffee and cakes.
- **Address:** 1024 Argyle St, Glasgow G3 8LX
- **Website:** https://thesteamie.co.uk/our-cafe

Did you know?

At 127 metres high, the Glasgow Tower holds the Guinness world record for the tallest, fully-rotating, freestanding structure in the world.

Image Credits

All images are either photos taken by the author or are in the public domain.

Bibliography

Books:

Beech, M. (2014). "Alpha Centauri: Unveiling the Secrets of Our Nearest Stellar Neighbor". Springer.

Burnett, A. (2010). "Invented in Scotland: Scottish Ingenuity and Invention Throughout the Ages". Birlinn Ltd.

Gladstone-Millar, L. (2012). "John Napier: Logarithm John". NMSE - Publishing Ltd.

Hirshfeld , A., W. (2002). "Parallax: The Race to Measure the Cosmos". Palgrave Macmillan.

Hockey, T. (2009). "Biographical Encyclopedia of Astronomers". Springer.

Lindley, D. (2004). "Degrees Kelvin: A Tale of Genius, Invention, and Tragedy". Henry (Joseph) Press.

Mahon, B. (2013). "The Man Who Changed Everything – the Life of James Clerk Maxwell". Wiley.

McHardy, S. (2013). "Calton Hill: Journeys and Evocations". Luath Press Ltd.

McIntyre, D., B. & McKirdy, A. (2012). "James Hutton: The Founder of Modern Geology". NMSE - Publishing Ltd.

Mitchell, A. (1993). "The People of Calton Hill". Mercat Press.

Rigden, J., S., & Stuewer, R., H. (2008). "The Physical Tourist: A Science Guide for the Traveler". Birkhäuser.

Tanford, C., & Reynolds, J. (1995). "A Travel Guide to Scientific Sites of the British Isles: A Guide to the People, Places and Landmarks of Science". John Wiley & Sons.

Scientific References:

Henderson, T. (1839). "On the parallax of Centauri". Monthly Notices of the Royal Astronomical Society, Vol. 4, p.168.

McIntyre, D., B. (1997). "James Hutton's Edinburgh the Historical, Social and Political Background". Opening address at the 1997 Conference organised by The Royal Society of Edinburgh celebrating Hutton's work on the occasion of the 200th Anniversary of Hutton's Death.

Schaaf, L., J. (2009). "Charles Piazzi Smyth's 1865 Conquest of the Great Pyramids". , History of Photography, 3 (1979), 331.

Warner, B. (2010). "Thomas Henderson and Centauri". Transits of Venus: New Views of the Solar System and Galaxy, Proceedings IAU Colloquium No. 196, 2004, D.W. Kurtz, ed.

Websites:

www.clerkmaxwellfoundation.org

www.glenlair.org.uk

www.curiousedinburgh.org

www.edinburghmuseums.org.uk

www.astronomyedinburgh.org

www.piazzismyth.org

www.camera-obscura.co.uk

www.roetrust.org.uk

www.roe.ac.uk

www.napier.ac.uk

www.open.edu

www.visitscotland.com

www.eeo.ed.ac.uk

www.dynamicearth.co.uk

www.famousscientists.org

www.digital.nls.uk

www.peoplemakeglasgow.com

www.scienceonstreets.phys.strath.ac.uk

www.glasgow.gov.uk/heritagetrails

www.physicsworld.com/a/in-praise-of-lord-kelvin/

www.universitystory.gla.ac.uk

www.glasgowsciencecentre.org

www.britannica.com

www.wikipedia.org

.

Printed in Great Britain
by Amazon

78951228R00051